DEAR YOUNGER

Me:

CAREER WISDOM FROM
WOMEN WHO'VE BEEN THERE

*Career Advice Every
Woman Should Hear Early*

RITA F. DAVIS, PHD

Preface

*D*ear Younger Me: Career Wisdom from Women Who've Been There is a guide for women embarking on their career paths. Growing up in a male-dominated world, we often face unique obstacles and challenges—especially in the workforce. While perceptions of women have evolved beyond traditional family roles, some still view our contributions through a narrow lens, seeing us primarily as nurses, teachers, or secretaries rather than doctors, administrators, or CEOs.

The purpose of this book is to provide women in the early and even mid-stages of their careers with insights that can help them navigate their professional journeys. It is informed by a study of numerous everyday women who encountered significant obstacles and, more importantly, how they overcame them. Their experiences, lessons, and resilience form the foundation of this guide—offering both practical advice and encouragement to the next generation of women leaders.

Acknowledgements

I wish to express my deepest gratitude to the seventeen participants who generously took the time and effort to share their insights with their younger selves. Reflecting on one's journey can be challenging, yet also deeply therapeutic, as it allows one to recognize the value created and the richness of a career well lived. Thank you to these courageous women for their honesty and wisdom.

I am sincerely grateful for the guidance and support of Dr. Jeffrey Magee. He was a guiding light when I struggled with this manuscript, and his encouragement never wavered. I also appreciate his recommendation and introduction to an exceptional editor who helped bring this book to fruition.

To my editor, Sheryl Green, thank you for your patience and dedication throughout this process. Your thoughtful and precise suggestions greatly enhanced this book, and I am truly appreciative of your expertise.

Thank you to Mrs. Hitchens for your input, encouragement, and steadfast support. You listened to my frustrations when responses were slow to arrive, celebrated with me when progress flowed, and lifted my spirits when this project felt like nothing more than a pipe dream. Your belief in me made a meaningful difference.

Without the unwavering support and wisdom of my spouse, this project would never have gained momentum. Your constant encouragement reminded me that I could accomplish the vision that came to me late one night in February 2025. You pushed me forward when I doubted myself, and your belief in me never faltered. Thank you for your endless support.

Lastly, I honor my late mother, who demonstrated every day what it meant to persevere through adversity and show resilience in the face of setbacks. She may not have known how profoundly her example influenced me, or how she served as a guiding light for so many women, but her legacy lives on through this work.

Table of Contents

Chapter 4 – Mentorship, Support & Empowering Relationships 81

Purpose: To highlight how connection, community, and guidance unlock opportunities that hard work alone cannot.

Purpose: To remind women that success is not defined by output but by a life that nurtures health, joy, and wholeness.

Purpose: To reinforce that character is a true measure of success and that leading with heart is a powerful advantage.

Encouraging today's young women to honor their journey, trust their voice, and continue writing their own version of success.

Introduction

The impetus for this book was my desire to look back on my career and determine whether I had fulfilled my potential. What were the issues and events that created success, and what were the things that got in my way?

I wonder whether my decisions would have been different if I had *only known then what I know now.* This phrase captures the idea that the knowledge we gain through experience would have been immensely helpful earlier in our careers. The challenge, however, is that wisdom often comes through trial and error – what we recognize as experience.

Looking back on my career, I did not know where or how to find the career advice I needed. Identifying a trusted mentor who could provide meaningful advice felt overwhelming and, at times, impossible. To whom should I turn? Who can I trust? Without the right guidance, navigating my career decisions seemed like searching for light in the dark.

I heard a song by Brad Paisley, "Letter to Me." The song was about sending a letter back to his teenage self and offering advice on negotiating his high school years. It struck a chord, so I sat down and wrote my own career advice letter to my younger self.

This letter helped me realize that, while my career was successful, it could have been so much more. I did not feel I had enough knowledge or experience (alone) to give advice to today's young careerists. I wondered if I could find other women who would share their insights and knowledge with individuals seeking advice and answers on their career journey. Could I find the knowledge and advice that could have helped my career and would be beneficial to today's career women?

I invited fifty women to write career advice to their younger selves. Many of these women I have worked with throughout my career. Some were recommended to me by friends and family members. These were everyday working women—the kind you'd recognize in your own life: your mom, your grandma, your aunt, your cousin, your neighbor, your best friend. They weren't famous; they were real, relatable women, just like you and me. All these women were either retired or currently still working in their chosen careers. I solicited their insights and advice to provide a beacon of light for women who were just beginning or still navigating their careers.

Out of the fifty accepted invitations, I received seventeen letters. This request was not an easy assignment. Many individuals reported that the reflection on their journey was difficult. Many accepted the challenge but found they could not write a letter. Several women found this self-reflection cleansing and rewarding. They indicated it gave them the opportunity to stop and look at what they had accomplished rather than focusing only on what still needed to be done.

Each letter provides insight into these women's career journeys. They are reflections of the moments in their careers that shaped and molded their lives. I believe the best way to honor and respect these women's submissions is to present their letters exactly as they were written—in their original form. By sharing their words and stories unchanged, we allow them to offer career advice to their younger selves in their own authentic voices. This book presents these letters with the following themes:

1. Self-Belief, Self-Trust, Confidence & Perseverance
2. Growth Through Reflection, Curiosity, & Intentional Choice
3. Resilience & Acceptance in Your Career Journey
4. Mentorship, Support, & Empowering Relationships
5. Balance, Well-Being, & Identity Beyond Work
6. Integrity, Kindness, & Humility in Leadership and Growth.

This book would not be possible without these women stepping forward to provide their insights, experiences, and knowledge. It is their willingness to reach-back and help others that has truly humbled my experience with this project. My hope is that this book helps someone find the light I was searching for earlier in my career.

How to Use This Book

Each chapter has a worksheet or an exercise to help you reflect or move forward. Please grab your favorite notebook, your beverage of choice, and take the time to reflect on the past and your future. Your future self will thank you for it.

You can find worksheets and other resources at www.WomensCareerWisdom.com.

CHAPTER 1

Self-Belief, Self-Trust, Confidence & Perseverance

Trusting Yourself

Your life changes the moment you decide to trust the quiet wisdom within you more than the noise around you.

Letters

GINGER:

Trusting Yourself and Owning Your Power

RITA:

Believing in Your Strength and Showing Up Anyway

BOBBIE-SUE:

Overcoming Adversity Through Perseverance

Ginger

Trusting Yourself and Owning Your Power

*G*inger encourages her younger self to trust intuition, stay authentic, and make choices aligned with her personal values rather than external pressures. She emphasizes protecting mental and emotional well-being, maintaining healthy family and social relationships, and not rushing life milestones (like a relationship or children) until the time feels right. She advises prioritizing health, setting boundaries, saving money early, and being cautious with trust. She stresses patience, resilience, and faith in oneself while embracing life as a journey of growth.

Here is Ginger's advice letter to her younger self:

Dear Younger Me,

Trust your instincts—your spirit, or what others may call your gut feeling. Block out the noise and distractions around you. Stay true to yourself and make decisions that feel right to you. You are the captain of your own ship. Some days, the waters will be calm; other days, they'll be choppy or rough. But no matter the conditions, remember that you have the strength to navigate through them.

Cherish your family, especially your mother and father. Appreciate the love they give you, but never allow anyone—family included—to cause you stress or disrespect you. Family should be a source of support, not turmoil. If something or someone costs your peace, it's simply too much. Protect your mental and emotional well-being at all costs.

Don't let anyone pressure you into finding a partner or having children before you're ready. What is meant for you will come in its own time. Trust that life will unfold as it should and move at your own pace. Always remember to respect yourself—your worth is not defined by anyone else's expectations or timeline.

Choose your friends wisely. Surround yourself with people who uplift, support, and challenge you to be the best version of yourself. Never forget to take care of your mental and physical health, for your well-being is the foundation of everything else in life.

Save your money early and be financially disciplined. The freedom it will bring later in life is priceless. Show grace to others, but always hold your ground. Your boundaries are important, and you don't have to compromise them to please anyone.

And above all, don't be too quick to trust others. Trust must be earned, not freely given. Take your time, build meaningful relationships, and know that not everyone has your best interests at heart.

Life is a journey—be patient with yourself and understand that growth takes time. Move forward, step by step, and know that you're capable of more than you can imagine.

Above all, trust that every step you take brings you closer to the life you're meant to live. Embrace your journey and know that the best is yet to come. Keep moving forward with faith in yourself—you have everything you need to succeed.

Rita

Believing in Your Strength and Showing Up Anyway

*R*ita reassures her younger self that despite early struggles, fears, and insecurities, everything will work out well. She reminds her younger self that those feelings of inadequacy and fear of failure were unfounded, as she would ultimately rise to become a Finance Director for a nonprofit organization and would build a successful, fulfilling career.

Rita offers heartfelt advice: believe in yourself, invest in lifelong learning, and view mistakes as opportunities for growth. She emphasizes authenticity, perseverance, and maintaining a positive outlook even in difficult times. Her message encourages self-compassion, resilience, and confidence in one's own worth and potential.

Here is Rita's advice letter to her younger self:

Dear Younger Me,

I am writing this letter to reassure you that everything will turn out okay. I know you often feel insecure and fearful about what the future holds, but trust me—the journey, though sometimes dark and challenging, will be worth your efforts.

I remember 1983 when you thought your world was ending. It felt like everything you had dreamed of and worked for was suddenly out of reach. Your career was just beginning—you had a bachelor's degree in business, but struggled to find opportunities to apply your knowledge. Your first job after college was a clerical position that paid just above minimum wage, and career growth seemed unattainable in your local region. This is where fear and self-doubt held you back.

Your biggest insecurity was your lack of faith in your abilities. You feared that people would see you as an imposter or that one mistake would expose you as someone unremarkable. But let me tell you—those fears were completely unfounded. You will go on to spend the last nine years of your career as a Finance Director for a nonprofit organization. You have so much to give, and your accomplishments are something to be proud of.

Here is some advice to help you grow and succeed:

1. **Believe in yourself.** Don't be afraid to show your true self to the world. You are remarkable—never doubt that.

2. **Invest in yourself.** Education and continuous learning are invaluable. The knowledge and experience you gain will propel you forward.

3. **Don't fear mistakes.** While always striving for excellence, understand that mistakes are opportunities for growth. Just be sure to learn from them and avoid repeating them. (And yes, you will make your fair share of mistakes!)

Just as in 1983, there will be times when the world feels dark, and the road ahead seems endless. But you will find the light again and experience joy and fulfillment. Here are a few words of encouragement to guide you along the way:

- Remember what Robert H. Schuller said: *"Success is never ending; failure is never final."*
- If you make a mistake, own it. Never try to sweep it under the rug.
- Be your authentic self. Don't try to be anyone else.
- Keep learning, growing, and investing in yourself.
- If you find yourself dreading work, seek a new opportunity. Better yet, find your passion and follow where it leads.
- Don't absorb the negativity of others. Stay positive.

Lastly, be kind. Not just to others, but also to yourself. Kindness fosters joy and harmony in life.

Bobbie-Sue

Overcoming Adversity Through Perseverance

*B*obbie-Sue reflects on overcoming the effects of growing up in an abusive household and struggling with self-doubt and insecurity. Despite these challenges, she pursued her dream of becoming a Special Education teacher. Starting as a teacher's assistant with little pay, she found encouragement from a mentor to take small steps—like one class at a time—helping her build her confidence.

With persistence and determination, she earned a bachelor's degree (with honors), a master's degree, and had a 38-year career in Special Education. She emphasizes resilience, self-belief, and breaking cycles of negativity. She advises moving forward, taking small steps, surrounding yourself with positivity, and practicing kindness toward others and yourself.

Here is Bobbie-Sue's advice letter to her younger self:

Dear Younger Me,

Growing up in a very mentally and verbally abusive household, I know you don't think you're capable of much or that you have the power to change these feelings.

This is not true.

In 1986, right out of high school, you wanted to be a Special Education teacher, but you didn't think you could actually accomplish college (let alone afford it). Your first real job was becoming a Special Education assistant, which got your foot in the door. This was an important move. The pay was awful, and you wanted to be a teacher so badly, but once again, how could you go to college full-time?

In 1989, a wise lady once told me, "Why don't you just take one class a semester? You'll get to your end goal before you know it, one step at a time."

You didn't realize that was even an option because no one in your family had attended college before you. Fast forward 5 ½ years, and you did it! You walked across that stage and received your much-deserved diploma (with Summa Cum Laude at that). That scared, insecure young lady had accomplished something that she was told, over and over again, she couldn't do. You may have proved those people wrong, but more importantly, you've proved so much to yourself. You can be somebody just one step at a time. You see, you can accomplish anything because next comes your Master's and 38 years in the Special Education field.

You overcame the negativity and insecurity and broke the abusive cycle. I'm so proud of you!

My advice to you is never give up. Small steps forward are a lot more beneficial than just spinning your tires and standing still. You must believe in yourself and know you're never alone during your unique chapter of life. Yes, there will be times that you feel deserted and ready to give up, but remember, there are more for you than against you. Keep moving forward. You must also believe that you need to prove nothing to anyone, just to yourself.

Surround yourself with positive people; nobody gets to bring you down with negativity. Always be kind to others, but do not forget to be kind to yourself as well. You deserve that.

Just remember that everything will be ok and will work out. You are never given more than you can handle, one step at a time.

Reflection

WHAT'S THE MESSAGE:

Self-Belief, Self-Trust, Confidence & Perseverance

WORKSHEET:

Strengthening Confidence & Perseverance

What's The Message:

Self-Belief, Self-Trust, Confidence & Perseverance

---

*T*he message found in the letters from Ginger, Rita, and Bobbie-Sue is about **self-belief, self-trust, confidence, and perseverance.** But what do these messages really mean? What does it mean to truly trust your judgment or believe you have the potential and ability to succeed? Do you second-guess your decisions? Do you trust your instincts? Your gut?

Self-belief and self-trust both relate to your confidence in yourself, though they are not the same. **Self-belief** is confidence in your abilities, qualities, and potential. **Self-trust** is confidence in your judgement, decisions, and inner guidance.

Self-belief means trusting that you can make sound decisions, learn from mistakes, and face challenges while still valuing yourself – even when things don't turn out perfectly. It does not mean believing you are the best at everything or that you will never experience doubt. Instead, it means believing you are enough to try, to grow, and to keep going. It is the inner voice that says, *"I can handle this,"* or *"I'm capable of learning and improving,"* especially when situations feel difficult or uncertain.

Self-trust is confidence in your ability to rely on yourself. It means trusting your perceptions, values, instincts, and emotions – and taking them seriously. You do not dismiss your inner experience or assume you are wrong simply because someone else disagrees. Self-trust acknowledges that you won't always make the right choice, but it also trusts you to learn, adjust, and recover. Your decisions reflect what matters to you, not just what gains approval, avoids conflict, or meets others' expectations. Self-trust allows you to move forward without perfect certainty, knowing that clarity often comes after action, not before.

While self-belief and self-trust are rooted in looking inward, **confidence** often shows outwardly. Confidence is the belief that you can meet or manage a situation. It does not guarantee success or perfection, but it does mean trusting your ability to respond. You don't need certainty about outcomes. You trust that whatever happens, you can think, adapt, learn, and recover.

Confidence allows you to be seen. It gives you permission to act, speak, or try without excessive self-protection. It is emotional steadiness, not the absence of fear, doubt, or nerves. Confidence means you are not ruled by those emotions. Your self-worth is not on trial. You are no longer asking, *"Am I good enough?"* Confidence is acting without constantly auditioning for approval. It is knowing both your strengths and limits without shame.

Perseverance is the ability to continue showing up, especially when progress is slow, uncomfortable, or uncertain. It means staying engaged when motivation fades, results lag, or effort feels heavy. Perseverance is the capacity to recover after setbacks, mistakes, pauses, or discouragement. It is guided by values and purpose, not pressure or punishment.

Perseverance is not about pushing relentlessly or burning out. It is endurance with self-respect. It allows flexibility by adjusting your pace, your strategy, and your expectations as needed. You persist without shaming yourself or forcing yourself beyond your limits.

So where does perseverance come from? Not from constant motivation, but:

- Clear values and a strong "why"
- Realistic pacing
- Self-compassion during setbacks
- An environment that supports learning
- The ability to rest, reflect, and resume.

How These Qualities Work Together

- **Self-Belief** says: *"I can handle this, I'm capable of learning and improving even when things are difficult or uncertain."*
- **Self-Trust** says: *"I believe my inner signals and will listen to them."*
- **Confidence** says: *"I believe I can handle whatever happens when I act."*
- **Perseverance** says: *"I will keep returning to what matters, even when it's hard."*

Together, these qualities form a steady foundation—one that allows growth, resilience, and forward movement without sacrificing self-respect.

Career Reflection Worksheet

Strengthening Confidence & Perseverance

---

*U*se this worksheet to reflect honestly, track growth, and intentionally shape your career journey.

Self-Belief & Self-Trust
Self-Belief: How You See Yourself at Work

Redefining Competence

Competence isn't knowing everything. It's learning, asking, and following through.

Reflection

- What skills am I currently developing?

  _____

  _____

- Where have I learned quickly or adapted well recently?

  _____

  _____

Separating Performance from Identity

A setback is feedback, not a definition of your worth.

Reflection

- A recent challenge or disappointment:

  _____

  _____

- What skill or lesson is this pointing me toward?

  _____

  _____

- What would I do differently next time?

  _____

  _____

Visible Contribution

- How do I currently share my progress or impact?

  _____

  _____

- Where could I speak more clearly about outcomes or results?

  _____

  _____

Self-Trust: Honoring Your Word and Your Capacity

Keeping Commitments

- One commitment I consistently keep at work:

  _____

  _____

- Where could I speak more clearly about outcomes or results?

  _____

  _____

Decision-Making

- A recent career decision I'm questioning:

  _____

  _____

- What information did I have when I made it?

  _____

  _____

- What would it look like to stand behind this decision now?

  _____

  _____

Honoring Capacity

- Where do I feel stretched too thin?

  _____

  _____

- What boundary, resource, or adjustment would support me?

  _____

  _____

Feedback as Data

- Recent feedback I received:

  _____

  _____

- What is useful to apply?

  _____

  _____

- What doesn't align with my goals or values?

  _____

  _____

Confidence: Evidence Over Emotion

Your Career Evidence File

List of recent wins (big or small):

- _____

- _____

- _____

- _____

Stop Waiting to Feel Ready

- One opportunity I've been hesitating to pursue:

  _____

  _____

- What's one small step I could take this week?

  _____

  _____

Skill Growth

- One high-impact skill I want to strengthen:

  _____

  _____

- How will I practice or develop it?

  _____

  _____

Using Your Voice

- Where do I hold back in meetings or conversations?

  _____

  _____

- What would it sound like to speak up anyway?

  _____

  _____

Perseverance: Staying the Course

Anchoring in Purpose

- Why does my current role or career direction matter to me?

  _____

  _____

- What value or long-term goal does this connect to?

  _____

  _____

Breaking Goals Into Steps

- One long-term career goal:

  _____

  _____

- The next manageable step toward it:

  _____

  _____

Managing Setbacks

- A recent setback or obstacle:

  _____

  _____

- How can I reframe this as temporary or solvable?

  _____

  _____

Past Resilience

- A time I pushed through a challenge successfully:

  _____

  _____

- What strengths did I use then that I can use now?

  _____

  _____

Integration: Moving Forward Intentionally

One belief I want to reinforce:

_____

_____

One behavior I want to practice consistently:

_____

_____

One boundary or act of self-advocacy I will commit to:

_____

_____

My next clear, actionable step:

_____

_____

Remember: Growth isn't linear. Confidence is built through action, keep moving… one honest step at a time.

CHAPTER 2

Growth Through Reflection, Curiosity & Intentional Choices

Choosing Growth

Growth begins when curiosity replaces certainty, and reflection replaces routine.

Letters

KERRY:

Embracing Curiosity, Taking Smart Risk

RENEE:

Making Proactive, Purposeful Career and Life Decisions

ERIN:

Learning and Growing Through Every Experience

Kerry

Embracing Curiosity, Taking Smart Risk

*K*erry reassures her younger self, who feels lost after not getting into a journalism program, so she does not panic about the future. She emphasizes that careers are not built on perfect plans from the start but rather through curiosity, recognizing opportunities, and trusting her instincts. She advises that seemingly risky or backward career moves can ultimately lead to greater opportunities, self-discovery, and long-term success.

Kerry recognizes that waiting to return to school proved advantageous, as life experience makes education more meaningful and opens doors later in life. Ultimately, perseverance and strategic choices led to a fulfilling career in training and consulting, where meaningful work and independence were achieved.

Here is Kerry's advice letter to her younger self:

Dear Younger Me,

I know you're devastated that you didn't get into the journalism program since that was your plan throughout high school. I know you're panicking because you have no backup plan, and at 21, newly married and needing to support your-selves, you feel this crushing pressure to figure out what you want to do with your life right now. Everyone else seems to have it figured out, and you're terrified you'll end up stuck in some dead-end minimum wage job forever.

Here's what I want you to know: That feeling of being behind, of everyone else having a plan while you're floun-dering? It's an illusion. You don't need to have your career figured out to start building one. The path to work you love isn't found through endless soul-searching or aptitude tests. It's discovered by staying curious, recognizing opportunity, and taking strategic steps forward, even when you can't see exactly where they lead.

When you're working in a stable position, and you're offered a job as a loans clerk that pays less, you'll make the right decision by looking beyond the initial job offer at the career possibilities. Trust your instinct. You're not just taking a job, you're positioning yourself somewhere you can dis-cover what you're actually good at. That 'step backward' will become a loans officer position that pays better than what you left, and more importantly, you'll learn that although school was hard for you, you're actually fairly smart and you really enjoy the challenge of learning new things that are applicable to you.

Later on, when you have finally landed a full-time posi-tion, and you're offered a part-time entry-level position at a large organization, take it—even though you're giving up guaranteed full-time hours and security. You're seeing the career potential a large organization can offer. You will never work part-time, and within a year, you'll be offered three positions within the company, including your top choice as an instructional designer and facilitator in the new training unit. That's when everything clicks. When you discover you love designing training programs and are fascinated by cognitive science.

So that panic you're feeling about not knowing what you want to do? Let it go. You're going to build an amazing career not by having all the answers upfront, but by staying curious, recognizing opportunity, and trusting your instincts about potential (even when you can't see exactly where it leads).

And here's something else that will surprise you: waiting to go back to school will turn out to be one of your smartest decisions. When you do start that certificate in adult education, you'll have real experience to connect it to. Years later, that experience will be so valuable that you'll be able to jump directly into a Master's program and finish your degree in your 40s—something that never would have been possible if you'd tried to force the traditional path.

You're going to end up running your own business as a training consultant, working from home, occasionally traveling internationally, doing meaningful work that makes a difference in the world. People will say you're lucky, but you'll know better. You created it, one strategic decision at a time, and with a lot of perseverance.

Renee

Making Proactive, Purposeful Career and Life Decisions

*R*enee's advice is to start planning one's career early, especially if higher education or trade programs are required. She emphasized the importance of aligning career choices with personal passions while also considering financial stability, benefits, and long-term security, such as retirement. She encourages continuous learning, asking questions, seizing opportunities, and listening to others for growth.

Renee believes that successes should be celebrated, while failures should be seen as learning experiences that build resilience. Her message is to pursue a career path that balances passion, stability, and growth, while striving to be the best version of oneself and to enjoy life.

Here is Renee's advice letter to her younger self:

Dear Younger Me,

The decisions you will have to make in your early adult life will be challenging and can seem difficult. When choosing a career path, it would be beneficial to know as early as possible what you "want to do" in life. Try to prepare in high school or even middle school, especially if your career path involves college or further education.

Think about your passions and what makes you happy. A career is an investment in you and your future. Choose a career that reflects who you are as a person and also provides stability. You need both financial and emotional stability. Financial stability comes from your salary and benefits. Benefits such as low or no-cost health insurance, life insurance, vacation and personal days, retirement plans, and other miscellaneous bonuses can greatly supplement your personal finances. Look ahead and prepare for retirement. This is very, very important. Invest and take chances. When considering a career, remember the importance of these life-long benefits.

If your career choice involves college, start preparing in high school, as you can often take college courses for credit. Look into trade schools or programs! Once you are employed, learn all you can from "seasoned" co-workers. Don't be afraid to ask questions and take on projects. Take on every opportunity that is offered to you in life. Opportunities are once-in-a-lifetime chances; always take them. You won't have any regrets if you do.

Learn to work independently and to be part of a team. Listen to people, your friends, neighbors, old people, and even kids; they will all teach you things every day. Listen, Listen, Listen. Sometimes you will lead, and other times you will have to follow. You will have successes and failures. Celebrate each success, big or small. Accept and learn from the failures. You need to make adjustments and always come back stronger.

At times, your career will seem difficult and full of obstacles, but those obstacles build character and strength. Choose the path closest to your passion with the most stability and growth. Always strive to be the best version of yourself, but most of all, be yourself and have fun. Life is short!

Erin

Learning and Growing Through Every Experience

*E*rin reflects on the lessons learned throughout her life—the regrets, mistakes, growth, and gratitude that have shaped who she is today. She recalls missed opportunities, harmful choices, and wisdom gained from those experiences. Despite her regrets, she has found pride and peace in her personal growth—reconciling relationships, finding her voice, and continuing to grow each day.

Here is Erin's letter of advice to her younger self:

Dear Younger Me,

There are things I wish I'd done —
like telling someone what I really felt,
taking the LSATs when I had the chance,
starting to invest when time was on my side.
I wish I'd spent more hours trying to understand my mother,
and fewer staying loyal to jobs that led nowhere.
I wish I'd studied the quiet language of trauma sooner,
learned the guitar just for the joy of it,
been gentler with other people's hearts,
and spoken up for my brother with more strength than fear.

There are things I wish I hadn't done —
tangled myself in codependent love stories
with people who fed on chaos,
romanticized the danger, the "glamour," of being close to power.
I gave too many chances to the unfaithful,
chased quick fixes when what I needed was patience,
experimented too curiously with escape,
and burned my skin and my spirit a few too many times.
I bought cars that broke down as easily as some of my dreams.

And yet—
I am glad.

Glad I bought real estate early,
built something solid beneath my feet.
Glad I never stopped learning,
that I took Constitutional Law seriously
and found my voice — sometimes singing,
sometimes speaking for those who couldn't.
I'm proud I quit smoking,
reconciled with my mother before she was gone,
forgave the others,
and built a relationship where trust is not a wish,
but a practice.

I am glad that my heart, though scarred, is still grateful —
and that I keep reinventing myself,
examining, rebuilding, forgiving,
growing into the kind of woman
who can look back and say:

I learned. And I'm still learning.

Reflection

WHAT'S THE MESSAGE:

Creating Growth with Intention

WORKSHEET:

Reflection, Curiosity & Choice-Making

What's The Message:

Creating Growth with Intention

---

*T*he letters from Kerry, Renee, and Erin remind us of something powerful: career growth doesn't just **happen**...we build it. It takes reflection, curiosity, and intentional choices. When we practice these consistently, we learn from our experiences, discover what excites us, and make decisions that move us closer to the career we want. It sounds simple, but staying focused and purposeful can be surprisingly hard.

Reflection isn't just looking back. It's understanding what our experiences are trying to teach us. It means slowing down long enough to ask ourselves:

- What actually happened here?
- Why did it play out that way?
- What does that tell me about what I want next?

When we reflect, we review the moments that shaped us—the wins, the frustrations, the feedback that stuck with us. We try to notice patterns: Where do I shine? What still challenges me? What kind of work gives me energy... and what drains it?

Reflection helps us to understand ourselves, *our strengths, our values, and our motivations.* Without reflection, we're just checking days off a calendar. With it, every experience becomes progress.

Try asking yourself questions like:

- What am I proud of this week?
- What would I do differently next time?
- What am I getting better at? Where do I need support?
- Which tasks felt meaningful or exciting?

Curiosity is that spark inside that makes us want to learn more, ask why, and explore what else is possible. It's choosing not to settle into autopilot. Curiosity sounds like:

- *What does that team actually do?*
- *Could I learn that skill?*
- *What if I tried something new?*

It encourages us to experiment: to volunteer for a project that scares you a little, reach out to someone in a role you're curious about, or take a course just because it interests you. Curiosity keeps your career alive and full of possibilities.

Intentional choices are where everything comes together. This is you deciding what you want and taking steps that point you in that direction. It means:

- Setting goals that actually excite you
- Choosing work that helps you grow in the right direction

- Saying "yes" with purpose and saying "no" when something isn't aligned
- Being proactive about opportunities instead of waiting for them to show up

When you choose with intention, you're not just moving forward, you're moving forward on the path that's right for you.

Here's how Reflection, Curiosity, and Intentional Choices work together:

- Reflection helps you grow from what you've done.
- Curiosity encourages you to explore what's possible.
- Intentional choices help you build the path to where you're going.

Career Reflection Worksheet

Reflection, Curiosity, & Decision-Making

---

*U*se this worksheet to reflect honestly, track growth, and intentionally shape your career journey.

Career Reflection – Understanding Yourself

Purpose: establish an honest baseline

Current Snapshot

My current career situation (role, studies, transition, pause, etc.)

_____

_____

On a scale of 1-10, how aligned does my current situation feel? _____

What's occupying most of your mental energy right now at work/career?

_____

_____

Energy & Engagement Audit

List 3 activities that energized you recently:

- _____
- _____
- _____
- _____

List 3 activities that drained you:

- _____
- _____
- _____
- _____

Strengths, Skills, and Use

Skills I use most often:

_____

_____

Skills I enjoy using the most:

_____

_____

Skills I want to develop more intentionally:

_____

_____

Where is there a mismatch between skill use and enjoyment?

_____

_____

_____

_____

Value Check

Circle your top **5 values (or add in your own)**:

Autonomy · Stability · Growth · Impact · Creativity · Flexibility · Learning · Recognition · Collaboration · Financial Security · Purpose · Leadership

_____ _____ _____ _____

Which **2 values matter most right now?**

How well is my current situation honoring them?

☐ Not at all ☐ Poorly ☐ Somewhat ☐ Well ☐ Very Well

Career Curiosity – Expanding Possibilities

Fascination Finder

Answer quickly:

Topics I explore "just because":

_____

_____

Problems I enjoy thinking about:

_____

_____

Conversations that energize me:

_____

_____

What themes keep showing up?

_____

_____

Adjacent Possibilities

My current field or role:

_____

_____

List **3 roles or paths one step away** from this:

- _____

- _____

- _____

- _____

What specifically intrigues me about each?

_____

_____

_____

Assumption Check

Complete the sentences:

"I'm curious about _____, but I assume
_____."

"Exploring _____ feels risky because
_____."

What assumptions could be **tested**?

Curiosity Micro-Experiments

Choose **1-2 low-risk experiments** (2-4 weeks max):

- ☐ Informational interview
- ☐ Short course/workshop
- ☐ Side or volunteer project
- ☐ Shadowing/observation
- ☐ Reading deep dive
- ☐ Community or meetup

Describe one experiment clearly:

- What I'll do:

  _____

- Time commitment:

  _____

- What I want to learn:

  _____

Intentional Choices – Deciding with Clarity

Directional Clarity

Right now, I want to move **toward:**

_____

_____

And move **away from:**

_____

_____

What I am not deciding yet (and don't need to):

_____

_____

Decision Criteria (Your Pre-Decision Filter)

Non-Negotiables (must-haves):

- _____

- _____

Strong preferences:

- _____

- _____

Nice to have:

- _____

- _____

Trade-Off Awareness

If I pursue what I'm curious about, what am I choosing to say no to with my time, energy, and attention?

_____

_____

If I stay where I am, I may be giving up:

_____

_____

Which trade-off feels more acceptable right now?

_____

_____

Fear vs. Misalignment

What am I afraid might happen if I change or explore more?

_____

_____

Is this fear mostly about:

☐ Uncertainty

☐ Identity/expectations

☐ Financial or practical risk

☐ True misalignment with values or energy

What signals point to **real misalignment** (not just fear)?

_____

_____

Future-Self Check

Imagine yourself **12-18 months from now:**

If I take a thoughtful step toward my curiosity, future-me will likely feel:

_____

_____

If I avoid change entirely, future-me might feel:

_____

_____

Which choice would future-me respect for being intentional?

_____

_____

Integration – From Insight to Action

Key Insights

The most important things I learned about myself:

1. _____

2. _____

3. _____

One Intentional Next Step

One small concrete action I will take in the next 7-14 days:

_____

_____

When I will do it:

_____

_____

What I'll pay attention to (energy, learning, resistance):

_____

_____

CHAPTER 3

Resilience & Acceptance in Your Career Journey

Embracing the Journey

Resilience is less about standing firm and more about learning how to bend without breaking.

Letters

LYNN:

Trusting the Process of Growth

LINDA:

Taking Chances and Committing to Lifelong Learning

KELLI:

Courage, Resilience & Self-Trust Along the Way

BECKY:

Flexibility and Acceptance Through Change

Lynn

Trusting the Process of Growth

L ynn shares her story of a nontraditional career journey filled with perseverance, pivots, and personal growth. She recounts starting her career at 17, working her way up to the corner office, navigating industry shifts, returning to school for a degree, and eventually finding long-term success in higher education as an Associate Vice President. She reflects on how life's detours, challenges, and unexpected turns all contribute to success and fulfillment when approached with perseverance, heart, and faith in oneself.

Lynn's key lessons highlight the importance of leading with passion, accepting that progress is not always straightforward, embracing opportunities even when they feel daunting, and trusting in one's worth and abilities.

Here is Lynn's advice letter to her younger self:

Dear Younger Me,

Let me start by telling you: everything is going to work out just the way it's meant to. You'll make some great choices... and some not-so-great ones. But if you keep an open mind and look for the lesson in every experience and situation,

61

there are no "bad" choices... just choices that help guide and shape your journey through life.

Two days before your high school graduation in 1987, you accepted a position that would become the foundation of your entire career—at just 17 years old! Much to Mom's disappointment, you didn't go to college right away. Spoiler alert: that's okay. Did it take longer than the traditional four years? Yes. But with tenacity, discipline, and determination, you earned your bachelor's degree in accounting in seven years, without college debt, and as a stronger, more focused student.

When you landed that accounting clerk job in 1987, you worked in a shared space with 20 other women on the finance floor. At the other end of the office sat the VP of Finance, in a beautiful corner office overlooking the corporate grounds. Even then, a fire was lit in your belly. You knew you wanted to sit in that office someday. And although you were never given the title of VP, you did land that corner office in 2000, thirteen years later. The path wasn't straight or obvious. It was built one step at a time by taking on more responsibility, showing up consistently, and being a true team player.

Then everything changed. The industry shifted in 2001. After two company bankruptcies, you transitioned to a new field—construction—where you gained firsthand knowledge of private industry finance. When the profits were up, it was great. But when the housing market collapsed in 2008, and payroll became a weekly concern, it was time to pivot again. You only spent four years with that company, but working under three of the owners sharpened your strategic thinking in ways you'll carry with you forever.

Fast forward to June 2025. You've just completed your 18th year in higher education. Though you initially took a step back (in both salary and title) the journey has been worth it. It took 10 years to build your reputation within this team, and now you proudly hold the title of Associate Vice President.

Here are some lessons from your journey:

- **Lead with your heart.** When your heart is your compass, the path unfolds naturally. Spend time reflecting on what *you* want. Not what your parents want, not what a partner might try to steer you toward. Do what makes your soul happy and your heart smile.

- **It's okay to take a step back to move forward.** The role you're in today is opening doors you never imagined. I'm writing this letter from the airport in Istanbul, after taking my son on a 10-day Mediterranean cruise to celebrate his college graduation. If someone had told me four years ago—on the day my divorce was finalized—that this would be my life, I wouldn't have believed them.

- **Fake it 'til you make it.** There will be days when you don't feel qualified or competent enough. Hello, imposter syndrome. But trust yourself. You've earned your place. Your reputation speaks volumes. You *are* capable, and you *do* belong in the room.

You got this, and you are worthy!

Linda

Taking Chances and Committing to Lifelong Learning

Linda presents an inspiring reflection on how courage, humility, and hard work can produce success that comes from determination, faith, and willingness to step outside one's comfort zone. She provides a glimpse into how she stepped out on faith to pursue a better life for herself and her family.

Linda reveals how taking risks and believing in herself were important in setting an example for her children. Her message is one of resilience and self-improvement. It's a reminder that it's never too late to take a leap of faith, work hard, and build a better life through courage, dedication, and love for what you do.

Here is Linda's advice letter to her younger self:

Dear Younger Me,

In 1985, I was a young wife and mother of 2 grade school-aged children.

I wanted my children to see me as a strong woman committed to making a better life for my family and to make myself better. (Life goals, keep bettering yourself.)

When I decided to return to school, it was after many sleepless nights and discussions with my spouse about finances, childcare, and the division of chores. We just decided to go for it.

I felt the pressure of the possibility of failure and of damaging our finances and family life.

It was a complete leap of faith. (Sometimes you need to take chances.)

After many years out of a classroom (other than being a class mom), it was very scary, exciting, and intimidating! Not to mention, I had to attend remedial math and English classes. Thankfully, I had my 5th grader to help me. (Set your ego aside.)

It can be humbling to be the "old lady" in a classroom full of newly graduated high schoolers. (Again, set your ego aside.) Not for nothing, but out of a class of 52 students. I was one of only three students to graduate... and the only woman! That's one of my proudest achievements! (Hard work pays off.)

I easily found work as a radiologic technologist. I continued to reach for more opportunities. I completed the requirements to become a certified MRI technician.

40 years later, and I'm still working. (As Confucius said, "Love what you do, and you'll never work a day in your life.")

Before earning my Rad Tech license and degree, I supported my family as a waitress. A noble profession that allowed me to provide a humble existence for us. Any work, no matter what, is noble.

And finally, I thank the people at trade and technical schools for providing an excellent opportunity for people like me who need an alternative to traditional education.

Teamwork does make the dream work!

Kelli

Courage, Resilience & Self-Trust Along the Way

*K*elli encourages her younger self to embrace life's journey with confidence, openness, and determination. She emphasizes taking risks, embracing opportunities, and stepping outside comfort zones for growth. She highlights the importance of mentors and relationships, resilience in the face of setbacks, and trusting one's instincts.

Kelli reassures her younger self that failures are valuable lessons and urges her not to wait for the "perfect time" to pursue her dreams. She inspires confidence in personal strength, resourcefulness, and the importance of enjoying the journey.

Here is Kelli's advice letter to her younger self:

Dear Younger Me,

I know you're excited about the journey ahead, but also a little unsure of what's to come. There will be challenges, unexpected turns, and moments of doubt, but trust me… each step will shape you into the strong, capable professional you are meant to be.

First, don't be afraid to take risks. The safest path isn't always the most fulfilling. Say yes to opportunities that push you outside your comfort zone, even if they seem intimidating. Growth happens when you're willing to embrace the unknown.

Second, find mentors and build relationships. You don't have to figure everything out on your own. Seek advice from those who have walked this road before you. Their wisdom will be invaluable, and one day, you'll be in a position to do the same for someone else.

Learn to navigate setbacks with resilience. Not everything will go as planned, and that's okay. Every roadblock is a lesson in disguise, teaching you adaptability and perseverance. Instead of dwelling on failures, focus on what they teach you and move forward with confidence.

Also, trust your instincts. There will be times when you doubt yourself, but remember, your intuition is powerful. If something doesn't feel right, listen to that inner voice. You are capable, resourceful, and stronger than you realize.

Finally, don't wait for the "perfect" time to chase your dreams. The right time is now.

Every experience, even the ones that don't seem significant at the moment, is preparing you for something greater.

Keep learning, keep growing, and, most importantly, enjoy the journey. You have an exciting future ahead, and you are more prepared than you think.

Becky

Flexibility and Acceptance Through Change

*B*ecky dreamt of becoming a teacher and a coach, but limited job opportunities after graduating from college forced her to reconsider her career path. While the U.S. Navy did recruit her for a promising career in physical therapy (as a commissioned officer), family obligations (especially caring for her grandmother after her grandfather's passing) kept her local.

Becky worked temporary jobs but finally found stable employment with the state government. This employment opportunity provided for financial security, growth opportunities, and eventually a strong pension and retirement.

Here is Becky's advice letter to her younger self:

Dear Younger Me,

As a pre-teen, you had dreamt of being a teacher and coach. After earning your bachelor's degree in 1973, your vision of obtaining that goal became unrealistic. All the jobs available in the local area had been filled by previous graduates. A new career prospect was introduced into your life. The US Navy was heavily recruiting you for their physical therapy program. It would be a career as a commissioned officer. This seemed like a great opportunity, but you had a dilemma. Your grandparents raised you and sacrificed a lot for you. Your grandfather had recently passed away, and you felt an obligation to your grandmother to stay in the local area and provide her care.

You may have heard the saying, "all things happen for a reason." After working a couple of temporary jobs, you were given a new career option. You were fortunate to be offered a job with the state government. The pay was fair, and the benefits were good. It allowed you to engage in a new career that would benefit you years later. You would rise through the ranks to become an office supervisor, which led to better pension and retirement benefits.

So, my advice to you is to be flexible in your career path; one door closes, and another opens. You will encounter prejudices and glass ceilings, but be prepared to address your concerns and present your attributes and assets to advance your career. Be flexible but firm in your decisions to pursue your dreams. Carefully weigh family and personal commitments and pressure as to how they will impact your long-term goal. Do what is best for you!

As you look back at your career, you sometimes wonder how things would have turned out if you had pursued a naval career. The peace of mind comes from knowing that your chosen career path turned out to be a good financial decision and very rewarding. You will also know that even if one thing had changed, you may not be with the person you married and have had a great relationship with for over 35 years. One decision can alter a string of events, some good, some bad. Stay true to your beliefs and morals and you will be just fine.

Reflection

WHAT'S THE MESSAGE:

Navigating Career Ups & Downs

WORKSHEET:

Practicing Resilience & Acceptance

What's The Message:

Navigating Career Ups & Downs

---

*T*he letters from Lynn, Linda, Kelli, and Becky collectively reveal a powerful truth: Career growth is rarely a straight line. Most of us don't move smoothly from one role to the next without detours, pauses, or setbacks along the way. Real progress requires resilience and the ability to accept that setbacks are not failures but are part of the journey.

Growth begins when you learn to make peace with where you are, even as you keep moving forward with intention.

Acceptance starts with recognizing that every career decision you made was based on the information, experience, and self-awareness you had at the time. You chose the best option you could as the person you were then, not the person you are now. Looking back with hindsight can make things feel obvious, but it isn't fair to judge your past through today's lens. Acceptance replaces self-criticism with compassion, allowing you to acknowledge your current reality without shame.

It also means letting go of the idea that there's one "right" career path. In reality, most choices don't lead to a single perfect outcome. Different paths come with different trade-offs, not better or worse lives. And while intention matters, chance plays a bigger role in our careers than we often admit.

Acceptance doesn't mean avoiding responsibility. It means shifting responsibility from punishment to wisdom. Finding peace isn't about denial. It's about being honest about mistakes, learning from them, and refusing to let them define your worth or limit what's possible next.

When you accept the past, it becomes part of who you are rather than something you carry like a weight. You can see how your choices shaped your values, strengths, and perspectives. You learn to hold both gains and losses at the same time, and you allow yourself to grieve what didn't happen without staying stuck there.

Setbacks—rejections, failures, wrong turns, unexpected changes—are painful, but they often become the moments that shape us the most. Career progress is rarely straight, and those disruptions can build resilience, clarity, and long-term growth rather than stopping you altogether.

Growing through setbacks means learning to see challenges as information, not verdicts. It's about building adaptability, strengthening problem-solving skills, and developing deeper self-awareness. Over time, this creates a career that may be nonlinear but is still meaningful and moving forward.

Resilience also has an emotional side. It's learning how to handle rejection, criticism, and uncertainty. It's managing stress, burnout, and disappointment. It's getting through layoffs, stalled growth, or career pivots without losing your sense of purpose.

And resilience means being willing to change. You update your skills as roles and industries evolve. You adjust your goals when life shifts. You stay open to new possibilities instead of clinging tightly to one plan you thought had to work.

At its core, resilience comes from knowing who you are beyond a job title. When you understand your values and strengths, you stop measuring your worth by one role, one employer, or one moment in time. You remember that you are more than your résumé, and you always have been.

Career Reflection Exercise

Practicing Resilience & Acceptance

---

*G*rab a sheet of paper and reflect on your career path with compassion, build resilience through setbacks, and move forward with clarity and intention, even when your journey feels nonlinear.

Reframe Your Career Story

List 3-5 moments in your career that felt like detours, pauses, or setbacks at the time:

- Moment:
- What happened:
- How it felt then:

Revisit each moment and answer:

- What did this experience teach me?
- What skills, strengths, or insights did I gain?
- How did this moment shape who I am today?

Reflection: Progress doesn't always look like forward motion. Sometimes it looks like preparation.

Practicing Acceptance (Without Self-Blame)

Complete this sentence for each career decision you regret or question:

"At the time, I chose this because ...."

- What information did you have then?
- What constraints or pressures were you under?
- What did you *not* know yet?

Now write a short statement of self-compassion:

"Given who I was then, this choice made sense because ...."

Remember: Acceptance is not approval; it's understanding.

Letting Go of the "Right Path" Myth

Check any beliefs you've held at some point:

- ☐ There is one right career path
- ☐ If I fail once, I've failed permanently.
- ☐ Success should look a certain way by a certain age.
- ☐ If I pivot, it means I made a mistake.

Choose one belief and rewrite it in a more flexible, realistic way:

Old belief:

New healthier belief:

Example:

Old: "If I didn't get promoted, I failed."

New: "Growth can happen even when titles don't change."

Building Resilience Through Setbacks

Think of a recent or significant setback (rejection, layoff, stalled growth, burnout).

- What happened?
- What story did you initially tell yourself about it?
- What *information* does this experience give you?

Now ask:

- What might this be preparing me for?
- What would resilience look like *right now*?

Emotional Resilience Check-In

Select any that resonates right now:

- ☐ Rejection
- ☐ Uncertainty
- ☐ Burnout
- ☐ Comparison
- ☐ Loss of confidence
- ☐ Fear of change

For one selected item:

- How does it show up emotionally?

- What do you usually do when it appears?
- What is one healthier response you could try next time?

Note: Resilience includes emotional care, not just endurance.

Adapting Without Losing Yourself

Answer the following honestly:

- My core values (top 3):
- Strengths that show up across roles:
- Parts of me that remain constant no matter the job:

Now complete the following sentence:

"Even if my role changes, I am still someone who …."

Truth: Your identity is larger than your résumé.

Moving Forward With Intention

Choose one small, realistic action:

- Skills I want to update or explore:
- Conversation I need to have:
- Boundary I need to set:
- Curiosity I want to follow:

What is one step you can take in the next 30 days?

Final Reflection

Finish this sentence:

"My career does not need to be perfect to be meaningful. It needs to be …"

CHAPTER 4

Mentorship, Support & Empowering Relationships

The Strength of Connection: Mentorship, Support, and Empowering Relationships

We rise higher when we rise together – through guidance, generosity, and shared belief.

Letters

DEBBIE:

Personal Empowerment Through Intentional Growth

VALERIE:

Learning to Trust Guidance from Others

SUSAN:

The Power of Female Mentorship & Genuine Support

Debbie

Personal Empowerment Through Intentional Growth

*D*ebbie acknowledges the challenge of pursuing higher education and professional goals without much family guidance or support. She recognizes that it takes resilience and determination to succeed.

Debbie's advice to her younger self emphasized the importance of finding mentors, creating and adjusting a focused plan, nurturing self-confidence, embracing mistakes and criticism as part of growth, balancing career with joy and relationships, and mastering communication skills. She encourages embracing the journey with flexibility, resilience, and a full appreciation for both professional and personal life.

Here is Debbie's advice letter to her younger self:

Dear Younger Me,

Looking back, I realize that sometimes having professional aspirations and ambitions made me feel a little lonely, especially when my family didn't really understand them or know quite how to encourage them. That doesn't mean there was necessarily anything wrong with my family... or with me. It just made things a little more challenging, coming from a family where higher education and professional ambitions were rarely discussed.

Looking back on my life and the challenges of putting myself through undergraduate and graduate school, and figuring out my own professional path, here is what I have come up with that I would tell my younger self.

- **SEEK OUT MENTORS** - Seek out the company of those who understand and encourage, whether they be teachers, businesswomen, family, friends, town leaders, etc. Many professionally successful women are happy to mentor, advise, and guide younger women. Don't be shy about asking if they will share some of their knowledge and lessons with you.

- **HAVE A FOCUS AND A PLAN** - Be clear in your own mind about your aspirations and goals. Write down your plan. Have specific goals, small ones and big ones, as stepping stones in your plan. Set an appropriate time frame for each one and celebrate when you achieve it! Be aware that you may alter your plan along the way. It's perfectly acceptable (even necessary) for your plan to have some flexibility. Perhaps one path may lead to another you hadn't previously considered. Or you may discover a passion or skill you hadn't previously realized. Adjust your plan along the way as appropriate. But make sure you have one. Keep it handy and look at it often. Stay focused even as you revise your plan. Because just winging it and hoping for the best will seldom get you where you want to go.

- **CONSCIOUSLY NURTURE YOUR SELF-CON-FIDENCE** and truly believe in your own abilities. Remind yourself that you can and will succeed. It's o.k. to get dejected, frustrated, irritated, or exhausted from time to time. Give yourself space to feel those things without self-recrimination. And then, sooner rather than later, pick yourself up again, remind yourself of your resilience, abilities, and determination, re-read your plan, and get back on the path!

- **DON'T FEAR MISTAKES, FAILURE, OR CRITICISM** - So much clarity and so many advances are made through mistakes and failure. Failure is not a reflection on you or your abilities. It is simply an unavoidable (and important) part of the journey. So, take the risks. Try something new. When it works out... great! When it goes awry, assess, learn, and move forward again. Along the way, listen to and consider *constructive* criticism from those who have your best interests at heart, such as suggestions for more efficient or more effective ways of achieving your goals and channeling your skills. Dismiss *destructive* criticism that seeks to diminish you or your abilities.

- **REMEMBER THAT LIFE ISN'T ALL ABOUT YOUR CAREER** - Take a break now and again and just have fun. Be silly. Laugh. Build solid and meaningful personal relationships and friendships. Cultivate non-work hobbies and interests. Even for the most ambitious, all work and no play is not a positive approach to life. As the old saying goes, "No one on their deathbed ever wished they had spent more time at the office."

- **BE A COMPELLING COMMUNICATOR** – I cannot stress this enough as I believe it to be critical. Confident and compelling communicators have a distinct advantage in all areas of life. Learn the power of using the right words, in the right tone, at the right time. That doesn't necessarily mean a lot of words... but the right words! Words that clarify, that use facts and truth, that have the power to make a point and to persuade, and that accurately express what you feel and believe. And remember that a key part of communication is listening. Learn to listen, *really listen*, and to respond meaningfully to what you hear. Communicating confidently, powerfully, and meaningfully, with conviction and clarity, is critical in both professional and personal settings.

So those are tips for my younger self as she navigates her educational and professional path and the path of life in general. Embrace the journey and live a full life.

Valerie

Learning to Trust Guidance from Others

*V*alerie shares how her life and career have been deeply shaped by the people she met and the advice, kindness, and opportunities they shared. She understands that not all influences have been positive, but the majority did guide her toward growth and success. She credits much of her progress to the encouragement and generosity of others, which humbled her and built her confidence.

Valerie believes that by being open about her goals and stepping out on faith, she found new career directions and adventures. She advises staying open, listening with both your heart and mind, and trusting that opportunities will come through connections and faith.

Here is Valerie's advice letter to her younger self:

Dear Younger Me,

Everything I hear and everyone I meet has the potential to impact my life in a meaningful way. Obviously, some of that can be negative, but more often than not, it has been positive. I am highly regarded by those I have worked with, and someone is always willing to give me a helping hand, a stepping stone, or advice that has furthered my career and my life.

No one achieves anything on their own, but I have found the interaction, helpful advice (sometimes to me, but often to others), and kindness of the people surrounding me have bolstered my confidence, humbled me, and moved me forward, even when I didn't know if that was the path I wanted to take. I step out on faith all the time (within reason).

I have always found it helpful to let others know what I want, even my long-term goals, and somehow I have been given help (spiritually and literally) in achieving them. For example, when I wanted to transition from my Nursing Career but was not sure of a path to take, a gentleman I met in the Air Force Reserves told me about an opening at Xerox where he worked, and I applied, got the job, and gained experience in a totally new career field. Then when I realized I wanted to do something different, I met a recruiter, a new friend, and he told me about an opening with a pharmaceutical company. I reluctantly took the meeting with the company, loved the interviewers, and ended up spending the next 24 years in a career I loved.

So, I guess my advice to my younger self is to always be open to listening with your heart and head as well as your ears.

Susan

The Power of Female Mentorship & Genuine Support

S usan reflects on her long career as a teacher, public relations director, and mentoring consultant. She focuses on what she has learned about women supporting women in the professional arena.

Over the course of her career, she noticed that many women did not act as team players and were often unsupportive or jealous when another woman advanced. This experience led her to discover the "power dead-even rule," introduced by Pat Heim and colleagues.

Susan regrets not surrounding herself with more female mentors who genuinely cared about her success, but was grateful for the one who did. She has since dedicated her career to teaching the importance of mentorship.

Here is Susan's advice letter to her younger self:

Dear Younger Me,

As I think back on your lengthy career as a former teacher, chief public relations director of an urban school district, and the last two decades as a successful consultant in mentoring, what have you learned that could be helpful to younger women? Sadly, there is one observation that has plagued your professional life. You trusted other women. Then you recognized that many women are not team players. They often seem jealous of others and are unwilling to mentor, encourage, guide, and support their female peers. You trusted only to find out that when you needed female supporters for advice as you were being promoted and moving up the ladder, there were few who were happy for you or wanted to see you succeed. Why is this? You didn't seem to experience the same with men.

Then one day, you got your answer. You weren't crazy after all. The problem is called the "power dead-even rule," a term coined by Pat Heim and colleagues in _Hardball for Women: Winning at the Game of Business._ This rule governs relationships, power, and self-esteem. For a healthy relationship to be possible between women, the self-esteem and power of one must be, in the eyes of each woman, similar in weight to the self-esteem and power of the other. In other words, these key elements must be kept "dead-even." When the power balance is disrupted (such as when a woman rises in status above other women), women may talk behind her back, ostracize her from the group, or belittle her. These behaviors are to preserve the dead-even power relationship that women have grown up with their entire lives. Of course, this is a subconscious process. Most women are unaware of this invisible rule and what drives their behavior, yet it is a reason women sometimes do not support other women. Remarkable!

You began thinking about all this. In looking back over your career, could you have done anything differently? You did have one female mentor who took you under her wing and gave you some excellent advice at one point. She genuinely wanted you to succeed. She was wonderful, unselfish, caring, and always in your corner. But now that you look back on it all, you wish you had even more female mentors like her. You know that the most important characteristic of a mentor is that they care about the mentee's career planning and personal development. You should have surrounded yourself deliberately with multiple successful female mentors who wanted to help, inspire, and encourage you, and be simply overjoyed when you listened to them, took their advice, and then succeeded, in part thanks to them.

Well, you do not have the answer, unfortunately, to obliterating the power-dead-even rule among women. But you do know that this finding has inspired you to spend a major part of your professional life teaching others not only about the power of mentoring but also how important it is to be a mentor, surround yourself with mentors, and be mentored. You preach it and teach it every day in your current career. You hope that other women are benefiting from your experiences and your teachings. You want them to know how important it is to help younger women succeed through their support and coaching. The good news: mentoring is a two-way process. It benefits the mentor as much, if not more than, the mentee. You continually remind young women on their early path to success: *Identify true female mentors and surround yourself with them. Identify the dead-even ones and discount them.*

You have just agreed to co-chair a women's affinity group for a well-known non-profit in your community. Each meeting will include a panel of experts on topics of interest to women. At the top of your list, addressing mentoring and the unique female dead-even rule. Perhaps the participants will offer solutions to avoid those dead-even women in our way!

Reflection

WHAT'S THE MESSAGE:

The Value of Community & Connections

WORKSHEET:

Building Supportive Career Relationships

What's The Message:

The Value of Community & Connection

---

*T*he letters from Debbie, Valerie, and Susan remind us of something essential: none of us succeeds alone. It's that simple truth we sometimes forget... we don't grow alone. We grow because someone showed up for us. Someone believed in us. Someone said, *"You've got this... and I've got you."* When women are supported, lifted up, and believed in, we rise higher than we ever thought possible. Mentorship isn't just a professional gesture; it's a relationship that changes who we are and who we become.

How Mentorship Really Looks and Feels

A mentor is someone who sees your potential even on days you cannot. They listen closely, help you think things through, and share what they've learned. They are not telling you what to do, but helping you steer your own path. They're the steady voice when you're doubting yourself. The person who shares a lesson from their past, so you don't have to navigate your future in the dark. They help you see possibilities you may have overlooked, and they remind you that your path is **your own**, and you're more than capable of walking it.

Mentorship gives us the reassurance that we're not navigating the challenges of career and growth alone.

Why Mentorship Matters So Much for Women

Honestly, many women have moments where they question whether they're *ready* or *enough*. Having a mentor in your corner can make all the difference. A mentor:

- Helps quiet the inner voice that says "you're not ready"
- Opens doors to rooms we haven't stepped into yet
- Teaches us how to handle bias and push through barriers
- Celebrates our strengths while helping us grow new ones
- Reminds us that we *belong* in leadership
- Gives us a living example of what's possible

How to Build a Strong Mentor Relationship

Here's how you can make the most of mentorship:

1. Reflect on what you want: confidence, clarity, new skills, etc.
2. Look for someone who inspires you and has walked a path you admire
3. Reach out bravely... most mentors are honored to be asked
4. Set shared expectations so both feel respected
5. Come prepared, stay curious, take action

6. Accept honest feedback as a gift meant to help you shine

7. Give back where you can. Gratitude builds trust and connection

8. Keep nurturing the relationship—it may evolve into friendship, advocacy, or partnership.

Mentorship becomes a relationship where you're not just learning – you're evolving.

Support Isn't Just Cheerleading

Support is more than encouragement. It's being present. It's someone sitting with you when you're uncertain and saying, *"You're not alone. Keep going. You matter. I believe in you, and I'm staying right here through all of it."*

It's emotional and practical. It's encouragement and accountability. It's someone who sees your worth even when the world (or your own thoughts) tries to shrink it. Support gives you the confidence to take risks, the strength to persevere, and the comfort of knowing you don't have to face challenges alone. It creates a sense of belonging in places where you may have once felt invisible.

Empowering Relationships

Empowering relationships remind us that you already have the spark... you just need someone to help fan it into a flame. These relationships are rooted in trust, mutual respect, and shared power. They encourage independence while giving us a safe space to grow, make mistakes, and rise again.

They say: *"You already have everything you need inside you. I'm here to help you see it."*

Why Mentorship, Support, and Empowering Relationships Matter

When women support women:

- Courage comes before confidence
- Confidence shows up before titles
- Our voices grow louder than our doubts
- Our voices are heard before a spotlight ever finds us
- Resilience is built through connection, not standing alone
- We rise, and we bring others with us.

Mentorship and empowering support are the threads that pull us forward. They help us build lives filled with purpose, leadership, and joy. Because when one woman rises, she makes room for others to rise with her.

Career Reflection Exercise

Building Supportive Career Relationships

———————

*G*rab a sheet of paper to plan and track actions to strengthen mentorship, support, and empowering relationships.

Step 1: Set Your Objectives

Question: What do you want to achieve through mentorship, support, or empowering relationships?

Action: Write down your goals (be specific and measurable).

Goal: Why it Matters. Deadline

Step 2: Identify Mentors, Supporters, or Empowering Contacts

Question: Who can help you achieve your goals?

Name Role/Relationship: How can they help you? Contacted? (Y/N)

Step 3: Plan Your Engagement

Question: How will you build and maintain this relationship?

Action Step: Frequency of contact. Resources needed.

Step 4: Set Expectations and Goals for the Relationship

Question: What are the expectations for the relationship?

Actions: Relationship Goals, Meeting Frequency, Key Outcomes Expected

Step 5: Track Progress

Question: How are your relationships helping you grow?

Actions: Date Action Taken, Outcomes, Reflection, Next Steps

Step 6: Reflect and Adjust

Question: What's working well? What needs improvement?

- **Successes/Wins:**
- **Challenges/Obstacles:**
- **Changes/Adjustments to Make:**

Step 7: Celebrate Progress

Question: How will you acknowledge milestones and achievements?

- _____
- _____
- _____

Tips for Doing this Exercise:

1. Fill it out at the start of a mentorship or development initiative.
2. Review and update regularly (weekly or monthly).
3. Share with mentors, peers, or managers, as appropriate, for accountability.
4. Use reflections to improve relationships and plan next steps.

CHAPTER 5

Balance, Well-Being & Identity Beyond Work

Reclaiming Yourself

You are allowed to step back, slow down, and reclaim the parts of yourself that ambition cannot define.

Letters

LOU:

Holistic Growth Through Balance,
Health & Relationships

CAREY:

Reclaiming Identity Beyond Work & Expectations

Lou

Holistic Growth Through Balance, Health & Relationships

*L*ou's letter emphasized the importance of a balanced and intentional approach to both career and personal life. Her advice includes nurturing your mind, body, and spirit; maintaining healthy relationships; exercising and eating well; seeking mentorship and collaboration; practicing loyalty; choosing a life partner wisely; and staying curious through lifelong learning.

The focus of her advice is on building a sustainable, fulfilling life and career while prioritizing health, relationships, and personal growth. Her letter underscores that true success comes from caring for yourself and others while continuously learning and growing.

Here is Lou's advice letter to her younger self:

Dear Younger Me,

Pay attention to your work-life balance

- o Nurture your whole self spiritually, mentally and physically
- o Maintain only healthy relationships
- o Choose your partner wisely

Exercise and enjoy good nutrition

- o Time flies, and without these two partners, you may find yourself unbalanced in life
- o Perhaps you will have made a bit of money, but you may not have put yourself in a position to enjoy it if you are unhealthy

Build great relationships

- o Find more than one good mentor
- o Collaboration is key when building yourself and your brand
- o Be loyal, model loyalty, demand loyalty
- o Follow leaders who serve and become one who does the same
- o Choose your partner wisely

Be curious

- o Life-long learning is a skillset
- o As age sets in, focus on what you *can* do rather than what you *can no longer* do

Carey

Reclaiming Identity Beyond Work & Expectations

*C*arey presents a heartfelt reminder to slow down, set boundaries, and prioritize personal well-being over the constant drive for achievement, approval, and perfection. Her letter to her younger self is a reflective and compassionate call to slow down, stop overworking, and release the need to please everyone.

Carey acknowledges her younger self's impressive accomplishments and work ethic but emphasizes that career, accolades, and social validation should not define her identity. She advises the priority of rest, joy, personal passions, family time, and self-care. She warns her younger self against unhealthy habits and burnout while encouraging boundary-setting, self-acceptance, and living a more intentional, fulfilled life.

Here is Carey's advice letter to her younger self:

Dear Younger Me,

Slow down, girl.

The problems will be there when you get into work tomorrow. The solutions will come to you in time. You don't have to muscle it out and work the most hours. You cannot

111

be available to everyone all the time. You need to take better care of yourself.

When you are the last to pick up your children from day care, stop it.

When you are at the grocery store at 10 pm for fresh raspberries, stop it.

When you rush from meeting to meeting, from work to volunteer opportunities, from doctor appointments to fundraiser galas, stop it.

Your life is so full. You have a lot of exciting things to do. You want to be invited to everything. You want to be the funniest person in the room. You want to be liked, loved, adored, and respected. You are. Don't work so hard to earn people's admiration. You are you. They will love you. Or they won't. Either way, it doesn't matter. You got your jobs because you are qualified and you are a doer. You are self-motivated, and you complete tasks with creativity and thoroughness that is unparalleled. You are an amazing employee! But it is costing you. Your job is not your life. Your job is not your identity. Your job is very important, but it is not you. I need you to understand that.

Turn your lens back inward. What brings you joy? Why aren't you taking horseback riding lessons every month? Why aren't you practicing yoga? Why aren't you visiting state parks with your kids? Why aren't you volunteering to help with events to raise money for causes you believe in? Because you are working too much. You are running the household. And you don't have help. There will always be only 24 hours in a day. Let's start prioritizing those hours differently.

You don't have to do it all. Women want to, and we want to be praised for handling everything so well. The house, the kids, the job, the husband. Stop it.

Your husband does not help you. That is a fact. He is not going to change for the better (spoiler alert—he gets a lot worse). You will try to stand by him and make him happy. You won't. That is ok. You had to lose yourself completely before you could find yourself more wholly. Some husbands and partners offer lots of support; others offer little to none. Unpacking the evolution of your marriage is something for yet another letter. For now, let's talk about you. And keeping you aware of what YOU need. What YOU do, and who YOU are.

I'm 53 now, and I subscribe to the "let them" theory, the "we do not care club," and countless solo travel blogs. I'm happily divorced and still working a lot. But I have stopped the stress, the chaos, and the search for affirmation outside of me. That is easy at my age—I am financially stable; I have amazing friends; I no longer worry about a social ladder, and I still work out. Oh, and for the record: YOU are NOT FAT. Your beautiful body is amazing. We can address body issues and confidence in another letter. For now, appreciate your strength, flexibility, and stamina. YOU have got it all, girl. Stay strong and exercise for all the mental and physical benefits. I thank you for that!

Yes, you started two schools in Delaware! Yes, you served on the boards of boarding schools, colleges, and historic homes. You were the volunteer of the year and the teacher of the year. Yes, you can be given a task and solve it in record time, with record numbers, and record under budget. You help others solve problems, counsel middle schoolers, and build endowments. You decorated a 1920s-themed event with live fish in vases on the tables. You change lives with kindness, intellect, and compassion. Your identity has become tied to these successes. You are scared that losing those accolades will make you lose yourself. What are you without those laurels? A lot, I promise you. You just don't know it yet.

How can you stay on your career pathway while also staying protected, nurtured, and happy?

Slow down.

When you are at work, you are worried about what is happening at home. When you are at home, you are worried about what is happening at work. This obsessive circling of thoughts will drive you bananas, and you will lose boundaries and balance. I want you to know that if you are not ok at home, you will not be ok at work. And vice versa. Prioritize yourself and your home life as much as you can.

Your work is a means to a better life. We all require a job for income and benefits. That is respectable and necessary! You want a job that uses your amazingly creative and capable mind. You want to make an impact on this world and leave a legacy. You are making our mark. You will be remembered. You just need to remember that a 40-hour week is normal. You do not need to arrive first and leave last. No one cares when you are there. The quality of your work is what matters. You do not need to work at home, on your way home, or even on vacation. Your clients and families will respect your boundaries. Set them. You do not need to be accessible to everyone all the time. It is respectable to leave work at home, so that when you are home, you can be with yourself and your family.

Do not allow yourself to work until you reach your breaking point. You cannot work so hard and just look forward to the vacation or girls' weekend as your rest. You must rest before you break. Take some time away from it all on a regular basis. Take the class. Read the book. Be alone. And not at

5 am when everyone else is asleep. Take the time you need regularly so that you can be the best professional version of you. Block out a mental health day every month if you can! Spend it with the kids, friends, or yourself. Do something that makes you inherently happy. Walk that beach. Paint that picture. Take that yoga class. Get therapy. It all works for your benefit and inherent happiness.

There are still social climbers and competitive coworkers surrounding you. Do not cave to their influence. It is hard not to try to keep up and compete. Try to remember: your employers will walk over your dead body to post a job opening on LinkedIn. YOU do not need to hurt your fundamental self to grow personally or professionally. Stay in your lane. Stay true to you. You will find friends who are loyal and important. You will have a job. Stop looking at what others have or are doing. You have so much to share. Don't give it all away.

And finally, some of your habits are putting you at risk. You do not need to be at the grocery store when it is dangerous to walk in the parking lot at 10 pm. You do not need to be the last person at work on Fridays. We can agree that you do need to have groceries. And you do need to use daycare. Just stop the attitude that you have to have everything everywhere, all at once. You are everywhere. You have everything. You do it all. Just slow it down a little. The raspberries will be there on the weekend. The kids will be able to play more at daycare tomorrow. And you will breathe easier, setting your priority inward. Start now.

Reflection

WHAT'S THE MESSAGE:

Protecting Well-Being & Staying Whole

WORKSHEET:

Prioritizing Life Beyond Career

What's The Message:

Protecting Well-Being & Staying Whole

---

*Y*ou and Carey's letters remind us of something important: life is more than just your career. Your job matters, of course, but it shouldn't define your entire life. True fulfillment comes from balancing your professional goals with your personal life... and from knowing who you are beyond work.

What does this message really mean?

Think of career balance like a seesaw. On one side is your work, on the other is everything else – your health, relationships, hobbies, and personal growth. Career balance is about keeping that seesaw steady. It's about going after your professional goals without sacrificing your happiness, well-being, or sense of self.

Why does this matter? Without balance, it's easy to feel overworked, disconnected, and defined only by what you do for a living. When you get balance right, though, you feel motivated, energized, confident, and satisfied both at work and in life.

Signs you might be out of balance:

Sometimes life gives you little red flags when work is taking over:

Physically: fatigue, headaches, tense muscles, stomach issues, poor sleep.

Emotionally/Mentally: stress, anxiety, irritability, impatience, feeling numb or burned out.

Work-related: long hours even when unnecessary, struggling to disconnect, missing personal events, feeling guilty for taking a break.

Identity: measuring your worth only by productivity, losing hobbies or creativity, feeling "lost" outside work.

How to create career balance:

Here's the good news: Balance is something you can actively create. Some key steps:

1. **Set healthy boundaries**: You can do your job well and still have time to rest and enjoy life.
2. **Prioritize well-being**: Work should support your health—not drain it.
3. **Have multiple sources of identity**: Your value comes from more than your job – friends, family, hobbies, learning, creating, and more.
4. **Grow sustainably**: Professional development is great but pace yourself to avoid burnout.
5. **Align work with values**: Your career should reflect and support what matters most to you.

Remember, work is a part of your life; it doesn't have to be your whole life.

What about career well-being?

Career well-being is about feeling healthy, fulfilled, and supported in your work. It's more than just having a job; it's having work that adds positively to your life.

Why does it matter? When career well-being is strong, you're more motivated, productive, less stressed, more confident, and better able to build positive relationships.

Here are some key ingredients for career well-being:

- **Purpose**: Feeling that your work matters
- **Enjoyment & engagement**: Being interested and satisfied with your tasks
- **Supportive environment**: Respect, fairness, and healthy relationships at work
- **Growth & achievement**: Opportunities to learn and progress without constant pressure
- **Healthy work-life dynamic**: Maintaining your physical, mental, and emotional well-being
- **Stability & security**: Confidence in your job, fair income, and manageable demands

Your job should lift you up, not wear you down.

Identity beyond work

Here's the truth: you are so much more than your job. You're a friend, a family member, a community member, a creator, a learner, and someone with unique passions, values, and traits. These parts of you exist no matter what your job is, and they make you who you are.

Why does identity beyond work matter?

- Career setbacks don't shake your self-worth
- Life feels rich, meaningful, and resilient
- You can change jobs, retire, or take breaks without losing yourself

Having a broad identity protects you from feeling like your value disappears if work gets tough.

How Balance, Well-Being, and Identity Work Together

These three ideas aren't separate; they feed each other:

- When your identity isn't tied only to work, balance comes easier.
- When life is balanced, your well-being improves.
- When well-being is strong, you show up healthier and happier in both work and personal life.

Bottom line: *Your career should support your life—not define it. When you cultivate balance, prioritize well-being, and nurture a rich identity beyond work, you'll feel more fulfilled, resilient, and energized in everything you do.*

Career Reflection Worksheet

Prioritizing Life Beyond Career

Use this worksheet to help you strengthen your balance, well-being, and identity beyond work. Use it for self-reflection, goal setting, and action planning.

Self-Assessment

1. Work-Life Balance

   - On a scale of 1-10, how balanced is your work and personal life? _____

   - Signs of imbalance I notice in myself:

     o Physical: _____

     o Emotional/Mental: _____

     o Work-Related: _____

2. Career Well-Being

   - On a scale of 1-10, how fulfilled and supported do you feel at work? _____

   - Areas where I feel strong: _____

   - Areas that need improvement: _____

3. Identity Beyond Work
   - List the roles and identities you value outside of your job:
     - ○ _____
     - ○ _____
     - ○ _____
   - Activities or hobbies that bring you joy:
     - ○ _____
     - ○ _____

Reflection Questions

Answer honestly to gain clarity.

1. What aspects of my job energize me?

   _____

   _____

2. What aspects of my job drain me?

   _____

   _____

3. What values and passions are important to me outside of work?

   _____

   _____

4. How would I like my work and personal life to feel in 6-12 months?

_____

_____

Action Plan

A. Strengthening Career Balance
- One boundary I will set at work (e.g., stop checking emails after 7 pm):

_____

_____

- One way I will create more personal time (e.g., weekly hobby, exercise, or family time):

_____

_____

B. Enhancing Career Well-Being
- One step to increase purpose and engagement at work:

_____

_____

- One step to improve support or relationships at work:

_____

_____

C. Expanding Identity Beyond Work

- One hobby or passion I will prioritize this month:

  _____

  _____

- One social or community connection I will strengthen:

  _____

  _____

Weekly Check-In

- My wins this week for balance, well-being, or identity:

  _____

  _____

- My challenges and how I will address them:

  _____

  _____

- Next week's focus:

  _____

  _____

Chapter 6

Integrity, Kindness & Humility in Leadership and Growth

Leading with Character

*True leadership is measured not
by the power you hold, but by the
values you uphold.*

Letters

TERRI:

Leading with Self-Awareness,
Integrity & Compassion

ALEXANDRA:

Gratitude, Mentorship & Staying Grounded

Terri

Leading with Self-Awareness, Integrity & Compassion

*T*erri reflects on her 42-year career as a radiologic technologist and educator. She traces her journey from an uncertain beginning at age 17 to a deeply fulfilling professional life. Although she initially "just picked" radiologic technology, her path evolved into a lifelong teaching career—something she had always wanted.

In her letter to her younger self, Terri offers thoughtful, experience-based advice: Always be kind, stay true to yourself, act on your ideas, and remain humble. She emphasizes professionalism, self-respect, and separating personal friendships from workplace relationships. She also advises embracing every experience as a learning opportunity, not worrying over small matters, and knowing when to let go and move on from the different seasons of life. Her reflections highlight gratitude, resilience, and the wisdom gained from a lifetime of work and human connection.

Here is Terri's career journey and advice letter to her younger self:

As I reflect on my 42-year career as a radiologic technologist, I wonder how I truly chose that career path at 17. I told everyone who asked, and then, eventually, my students, that I got an X-ray and I was inspired by that technology. However, in retrospect, I don't remember why I chose radiologic technology. Maybe I just "picked something" because it was what was expected. Like most girls, I wanted to be a teacher. Little did I realize that is what I would be for 42 years.

While working in a hospital setting as a registered radiologic technologist, I served as a team member, mentor, supervisor, and clinical instructor for our community college affiliate. Then, 26 years after my career began, I was hired by the Community College as the clinical coordinator and instructor for the radiology program. Finally, I am a teacher!

My career pathway began on Tuesday, July 5, 1977, the day I started "X-ray school". My career began when I graduated from "x-ray school" in June of 1979 and started working as a 20-year-old registered radiologic technologist. After a 42-year career in radiologic technology, I retired as Terri H RT(R) M.Ed. A career well "loved."

My career was a successful and rewarding journey, and I am proud of my accomplishments. If I had the chance to guide my younger self along the journey, what advice would I have after living through that successful career?

> *"All that happens to us, including our humiliations, our misfortunes, our embarrassments, all is given to us as raw material, as clay, so that we may shape our art."*
>
> Jorge Luis Borges
>
> *"Great people are just ordinary people with extraordinary determination."*
>
> Rick Warren

Dear Younger Me,

Let's start this journey together!

"Kindness *Matters*." Always be mindful that kindness matters in every situation and interaction. Be kind to all mankind. Remember that you really "get more flies with honey than vinegar." Always extend grace.

Be true to who you are...always! Listen to your instincts. Be prepared to defend your integrity, your decisions, and your reputation with respect and kindness.

Don't wait for things to happen for you. If you have an idea or plan, take action!

When you present an idea or a thought, be prepared and organized with an action plan. Remember that people will have different opinions, so be prepared to work with them. Remember, everyone's job is important.

"Don't sweat the small stuff," that will make the small stuff big stuff and cause unnecessary stress in your life. *"Worry does not empty tomorrow of its sorrows; it empties today of its strength."*

Every opportunity is a learning opportunity. Enough said.

Be humble. Humility is not a weakness; it is a strength.

Always be ***friendly*** at work. But don't play with the people you work with. Your "best friends" should not be the people you work with. True friendships should be beyond your work environment. This advice is hard to follow...be careful. Work friends come and go and will "dump" you when they've gotten all they need from you and move on to the next opportunity for them. Develop a small circle of true friends outside of work because those friends will always have your back and love you!

In life, it is important to know when a "season" is over. Learn from it, grow from it, cherish the memories, then let it go and move on.

Words to live by:

"It's not what happens to you that matters, but how you handle what happens." (Epictetus)

"Watch your thoughts; they become your words.

Watch your words; they become your actions.

Watch your actions; they become your habits.

Watch your habits; they become your character.

Watch your character; it becomes your destiny." (Laozi)

Alexandra

Gratitude, Mentorship & Staying Grounded

*A*lexandra reflects on nearly three decades in law enforcement to share lessons that would have been valuable earlier in her career journey. She emphasizes the importance of actively seeking mentors, saying "yes" to opportunities despite discomfort, practicing daily gratitude, and maintaining integrity in the face of challenges.

She describes mentorship as a vital force for growth, guidance, and resilience. She suggests social engagement, even for introverts, to build connections and open doors. She recommends gratitude and journaling as tools for resilience in a demanding career, and underscores integrity as the foundation of professional and personal character. Her letter validates past choices while encouraging intentional growth, resilience, and ethical strength.

Here is Alexandra 's advice letter to her younger self:

Dear Younger Me,

It is hard to believe you have spent 28 years in law enforcement. I remember being 18, wearing an auxiliary police uniform, trying to envision my life at 40. I have never had a distinct image of where I wanted to end up because I did not want to intentionally limit where life could take me. Now, on the edge of 50, I am reflecting upon the range of experiences I have lived. They have all brought me to some ideas I wish I had emphasized early on and more during our career.

I am only now coming to a fuller understanding of the important role mentors play throughout one's career. I have enjoyed the benefit of several mentors over the years, but it never dawned on me that these were relationships I should seek out and cultivate.

Find trustworthy people of good character whose style, talents or career paths interest you. Create a relationship of curiosity and appreciation as you learn from them. Good mentors understand succession planning. They want their paths of choice to persevere and inspire. Good mentors will help guide you while giving you room to make your own choices. They will celebrate your successes and help you understand your failures.

Mentors will change over the course of your development as you create your story.

Their influence is invaluable.

Mentors will push you out of your center of comfort… which brings me to my next suggestion. Say "yes" more often. As an introvert, you have not consistently viewed social activities as important. However, I realize I have missed out on opportunities for connection by avoiding situations that cause personal discomfort. Knowing when to push through that discomfort and say "yes" rather than retreat leads to growth. It might open doors you never thought existed. You will thank yourself later.

Gratitude is integral to maintaining a healthy outlook through your time as a first responder. You are going to see much that cannot be unseen, from amazingly touching moments to traumas you could not imagine. Intentionally finding at least one way to be thankful every day will keep your compass pointed towards resilience and recovery. Keeping a journal is a great way to chronicle your journey and to have a tangible record of your growth as you mature in your career. I wish that I had kept such a consistent chronicle of my story.

Finally, hold your integrity close. You will encounter various qualities of character both in your co-workers and community members. Expect your morals, ethics, and integrity to face challenges, sometimes in situations you may least expect. Be an impeccable example of these values and do not compromise your integrity for anyone. If you align yourself with quality mentors and continue to build your resilience, you will be primed to face these challenges when they arise.

This letter is not so much about regrets as about validating good choices. Choose to do the hard things now so you find satisfaction and peace by the end of your career. Seek out and engage the inspirational people around you to help guide your career. Intentionally identify glimmers every day to practice gratitude and truly appreciate your condition. Be the actions you want to see in others. And keep your chin up!

Reflection

WHAT'S THE MESSAGE:

Character as a Career Strength

WORKSHEET:

Practicing Integrity, Kindness & Humility

What's The Message:

Character as a Career Strength

---

*T*he letters from Terri and Alexandra highlight the importance of integrity, kindness, and humility in one's professional development. Terri emphasizes professionalism, staying true to yourself, treating others with kindness, and remaining humble. Alexandra advises holding your integrity close, reminding us that our morals and ethics will be challenged throughout life. Together, their messages reinforce that who we are matters just as much as what we accomplish.

Integrity

Integrity means being honest and acting in alignment with your values—even when it's difficult or inconvenient. It shows up when you keep your commitments, take responsibility for mistakes, make ethical decisions, and remain someone others can depend on.

Why Integrity Matters

- Builds trust. Trust is the foundation of strong relationships and leadership.
- Supports ethical decision-making over convenience.
- Protects and strengthens your reputation, opening doors long-term.
- Promotes self-respect because you know you're doing what's right.

Integrity builds trust. Trust is the foundation for career advancement.

How to Build Trust at Work

- **Keep your word**: Meet deadlines and communicate early if plans change.
- **Be transparent**: Share accurate information, even when it's uncomfortable.
- **Own your mistakes**: Focus on accountability and solutions.
- **Honor confidentiality**: Protect sensitive information and uphold ethics.
- **Be fair**: Choose what's right, not just what's easiest.

The impact of integrity on your professional growth: You gain respect, credibility, and leadership opportunities.

> "Integrity is doing the right thing,
> even when no one is watching."
>
> - C.S. Lewis

Kindness

Kindness means treating others with empathy, respect, and compassion—uplifting people and honoring their humanity. It encompasses treating others the way you want to be treated. It's expressed through active listening, offering help, showing appreciation, and communicating with care, even during conflict. Kindness is not a weakness—it's a strength.

Why Kindness Matters:

- Builds trust with others. It helps to establish trust and credibility that is essential for strong relationships and effective leadership.
- Strengthens collaboration and teamwork. People want to work with those who care.
- Creates a positive environment that fuels creativity, loyalty, and morale.
- Enhances emotional intelligence, helping you understand people and lead effectively.

Kindness is how you treat and uplift others with empathy and respect. It fosters collaboration, morale, and strong professional relationships. Here are ways to uplift and encourage others at work:

- **Show appreciation**: Regularly give recognition and positive feedback.
- **Listen actively**: Try to truly understand before responding or judging.
- **Offer help**: Be a resource when others struggle.

- **Communicate respectfully**: Be respectful even during disagreements.
- **Be patient**: Everyone learns at different speeds.

Kindness recognizes humanity in others
and acts with goodwill.

Humility

Humility means recognizing that we always have more to learn. It keeps us grounded and open-minded. Humble individuals ask questions, learn from mistakes, and uplift others rather than seeking all the praise for themselves.

Growth in humility includes:

- Being open to feedback and new ideas
- Admitting when you're wrong or still learning
- Celebrating others' successes without feeling diminished
- Leading through service, not through your ego

Why Humility Matters:

- Encourages continuous growth through feedback and learning from mistakes
- Builds stronger relationships by valuing others' contributions
- Prevents ego from blocking progress
- Makes leadership more relatable and inspires trust

Humility is about learning and growing. It helps to keep you from becoming stagnant. Here are ways to practice humility:

- **Ask for feedback**: Actively seek feedback and apply what's constructive.
- **Admit what you don't know**: Be willing to learn and ask questions.
- **Share successes**: Recognize team contributions rather than taking all the credit.
- **Challenge your assumptions**: Stay open to different views and new information.
- **Learn from everyone**, regardless of title or experience level.

The impact of humility on your professional growth: You get better continuously and build stronger team trust.

Humility is confidence without arrogance,
and strength without superiority.

When i**ntegrity, kindness, and humility** are combined, they become a powerful growth formula.

Integrity	Kindness	Humility
Builds trust	Builds relationships	Builds learning
Makes you reliable	Makes you supportive	Makes you adaptable
Strengthens leadership	Strengthens teamwork	Strengthens self-awareness

Together, they help you:

- ☐ Strengthen your reputation
- ☐ Build meaningful connections
- ☐ Thrive in collaboration
- ☐ Become a respected leader
- ☐ Grow sustainably and ethically

Integrity guides your actions.
Kindness guides your interactions.
Humility guides your learning.

These three virtues help you grow with purpose, respect, and authenticity – becoming someone who not only achieves success but also earns admiration and leaves a positive impact.

Career Reflection Worksheet

Practicing Integrity, Kindness, & Humility

Use this worksheet to help you build integrity, kindness, and humility at work.

Integrity

Acting with honesty, responsibility, and consistency—especially when no one is watching.

Self-Reflection

- What does *integrity* mean to me at work?

  _____

  _____

- Example of a recent moment when I chose the right thing, even if it was difficult:

  _____

  _____

- One situation where I struggled to be fully honest or accountable:

  _____

  _____

Action Plan

- One step I will take this week to strengthen my integrity:

  _____

  _____

Kindness

Treating every person with respect, patience, and empathy.

Quick Check

On a scale from 1-5, how often do I show kindness at work? (1 = rarely, 5 = consistently) ____

Reflection Questions

- How do my words and tone affect others?

  _____

  _____

- Who could use a little extra encouragement from me this week?

  _____

  _____

Action Challenge

- Do one small, specific act of kindness today: (e.g., thank someone, listen fully, offer help)

_____

_____

Humility

Recognizing strengths AND limitations, valuing others' contributions.

Self-Reflection Prompts

- A time someone else's idea improved a project:

_____

_____

- How do I respond when I make a mistake?

_____

_____

- How can I better acknowledge others' work?

_____

_____

Growth Step

- One thing I will practice this week to show humility:

_____

_____

Final Thought

Seventeen everyday women stepped forward and wrote letters of advice to their younger selves, transforming the challenges and darkness of their career journeys into a guiding light for others to follow.

These letters are like a hand gently placed on your shoulder... a reminder that you are capable, resilient, and worthy of becoming the woman you dream of being. They speak to the quiet uncertainty many young women carry, especially when standing at the crossroads of who they've been and who they hope to become. They encourage you to trust your intuition, to believe in your strengths even before you fully see them, and to give yourself permission to take up space in the world.

They remind you that confidence isn't something you magically wake up with. It grows as you do. It shows up when you speak for yourself, when you set boundaries, when you follow your curiosity, and when you dare to pursue what you love, even if no one else understands it yet. Every step forward, every mistake, every moment of courage contributes to the woman you are becoming.

These letters also acknowledge that life won't always unfold the way you expect. There will be challenges. Some will shake you, some will break your heart. But within those difficult moments live lessons that will make you stronger, wiser, and more compassionate. You are encouraged not to fear these experiences but to meet them with resilience and grace, knowing they are *part* of your story, not the *end* of it.

At the heart of this guidance is the belief that you deserve community—a circle of people who believe in you, uplift you, and remind you of your worth when you forget. Mentors, true friends, family, and even strangers can become guiding lights when the world feels dim. As you grow, these letters ask you to be that light for others, too. Empowering one another is how women rise together.

Importantly, these messages honor the fullness of your identity. You are not defined solely by what you accomplish or what others expect of you. You are a whole person with dreams, emotions, creativity, and a need for rest and joy. Taking care of yourself, your mind, body, and spirit, is an act of strength, not selfishness. You are allowed to choose peace. You are allowed to redefine success in your own terms.

Threaded throughout every letter is a call to lead with character: to be honest, even when it's hard, to show kindness without diminishing your own voice, and to move with humility while still celebrating your victories. These values shape a life that is not only successful but meaningful.

Ultimately, these letters offer a simple but powerful truth: you are enough, exactly as you are, and you are still becoming so much more. Hold onto your courage. Protect your tenderness. Walk boldly toward your future with your head high and your heart open. You are growing into a woman who will change the world simply by being yourself.

About the Author

*D*r. Davis earned her doctorate in Management and Leadership from Capella University, where her research focused on the characteristics of successful female transformational leaders. She is deeply passionate about understanding how leadership and management roles shape an organization's human character, particularly in relation to the growth and advancement of women's careers.

Over the course of her 32-year career, Dr. Davis has led teams at every organizational level. Her experience includes key leadership roles such as Finance Director, Partner, and Accounting Manager, as well as a variety of tactical middle-management positions. She has taught management and accounting courses at local colleges and universities, conducted numerous professional training programs, strengthened existing initiatives, and developed new programs for Special Olympics Maryland. She is a retired Certified Public Accountant (CPA).

Dr. Davis skillfully integrates theory with real-world application. Her diverse professional background spans academia, sports management, finance, the airline industry, and the mental health sector, allowing her to bring a rich, practical, and interdisciplinary perspective to her work.

Connect with her on LinkedIn: https://www.linkedin.com/in/rita-davis-phd-0a19312/

www.ingramcontent.com/pod-product-compliance
Lightning Source LLC
Chambersburg PA
CBHW070422290526
45791CB00005B/1793